AIRPOD PRO 2 USER GUIDE

Understanding the Key Features and Benefits

ALFRED T. WALKER

COPYRIGHT

Copyright©2025 Alfred T. Walker. All rights reserved. No part of this publication may be reproduced, distributed, or transmitted in any form or by any means, including photocopying, recording, or other electronic or mechanical methods, without the prior written permission of the publisher, except in the case of brief quotations embodied in critical reviews and certain other non-commercial uses permitted by copyright law.

TABLE OF CONTENTS

COPYRIGHT 1

TABLE OF CONTENTS 2

INTRODUCTION 4

    Apple AirPods Pro 2 4

CHAPTER 1 13

    Getting Started with Your AirPods Pro 2 13

CHAPTER 2 23

    Understanding the Key Features of AirPods Pro 2 . 23

CHAPTER 3 35

    Managing Battery Life and Charging for AirPods Pro 2 35

CHAPTER 4 45

    Advanced Features and Customizations for AirPods Pro 2 45

CHAPTER 5 57

Exploring the Health Features of AirPods Pro 2 57

CHAPTER 6 69

Troubleshooting and Care for AirPods Pro 2 69

CHAPTER 7 82

Accessory Guide for AirPods Pro 2 82

CHAPTER 8 93

Getting the Most Out of Your AirPods Pro 2 93

CONCLUSION 106

AirPods Pro 2 106

INTRODUCTION

Apple AirPods Pro 2

The Apple AirPods Pro 2 are a remarkable step forward in the evolution of wireless earbuds. Building on the success of their predecessors, the first-generation AirPods Pro, Apple has made significant improvements in sound quality, comfort, and features. Designed to appeal to users who demand the best in audio performance and convenience, the AirPods Pro 2 deliver a premium listening experience that seamlessly integrates with Apple's ecosystem.

Overview of the AirPods Pro 2

The AirPods Pro 2 are the latest iteration of Apple's truly wireless earbuds, designed with both audiophiles and casual users in mind. Since the release of the first-generation AirPods Pro, Apple has made various enhancements to ensure that the AirPods Pro 2 are considered one of the top-tier audio accessories for iPhone users.

What Makes the AirPods Pro 2 Stand Out from the First-Generation AirPods Pro

While the first-generation AirPods Pro were revolutionary in terms of active noise cancellation (ANC) and sound quality, the AirPods Pro 2 elevate these features to new heights. The key areas of improvement include:

Improved Sound Quality: The AirPods Pro 2 are equipped with a new H2 chip that enhances sound clarity, improves bass response, and provides a more immersive audio experience. The tuning of the drivers has been optimized to deliver high-fidelity sound across a wide frequency range, providing users with a richer and more detailed listening experience.

Enhanced Active Noise Cancellation (ANC): The ANC feature has been significantly upgraded in the AirPods Pro 2, offering up to twice the noise reduction of the previous model. This improvement ensures that users can enjoy their music, podcasts, or calls without distractions, even in noisy environments like public transportation or crowded cafes.

Personalized Spatial Audio: The AirPods Pro 2 include personalized spatial audio, which uses dynamic head tracking to create a surround-sound experience tailored to each individual user. This means that the sound will feel more natural and immersive, as if it's coming from all around you, regardless of your head position.

Better Transparency Mode: The Transparency Mode in the AirPods Pro 2 has also received a significant update. It now features Adaptive Transparency, which intelligently adjusts the level of ambient sound you hear based on your surroundings. Whether you're walking on a busy street or sitting in a quiet room, the AirPods Pro 2 will ensure that you hear the right amount of environmental noise without compromising the clarity of your audio.

Longer Battery Life: One of the most appreciated improvements in the AirPods Pro 2 is the extended battery life. With up to six hours of listening time with ANC on, users can enjoy their favourite content for longer periods without needing to recharge. The charging case provides multiple additional charges, allowing for a total of up to 30 hours of use on a single charge.

Enhanced Comfort and Fit: Apple has refined the design of the AirPods Pro 2 to provide a better, more secure fit for a wide range of ear shapes. With four different sizes of silicone ear tips, users can achieve a snug fit that not only improves sound isolation but also enhances comfort for long listening sessions.

Key Features: Active Noise Cancellation (ANC), Transparency Mode, Spatial Audio, and More

Active Noise Cancellation (ANC): Active Noise Cancellation is one of the standout features of the AirPods Pro 2. ANC uses built-in microphones to detect external sounds, which are then cancelled out with opposing sound waves. This technology allows you to immerse yourself fully in your audio, blocking out distractions such as traffic noise, chatter, or the hum of an airplane engine. The AirPods Pro 2 offer improved ANC performance over their predecessors, making them ideal for users who need a quiet environment for work or travel.

Transparency Mode: Unlike traditional noise-cancelling headphones, Transparency Mode lets you hear the world around you while still enjoying your music or calls. The AirPods Pro 2 take this to the next level with Adaptive Transparency, which automatically adjusts the amount of ambient sound you hear based on your surroundings. This feature is especially useful when you need to stay aware of your environment, such as when crossing the street or engaging in a conversation without removing your earbuds.

Spatial Audio: Spatial Audio with dynamic head tracking creates an immersive listening experience by simulating surround sound. With the AirPods Pro 2, Spatial Audio has been fine-tuned to provide an even more realistic and accurate soundstage. By tracking the movement of your head, the sound field adjusts dynamically to ensure that you hear the audio as if it were coming from the right position, no matter how you turn your head.

Personalized Sound: The AirPods Pro 2 are designed to adapt to your unique ear shape. Using the Apple Health app, you can perform an ear scan to create a personalized sound profile. This ensures that your listening experience is tailored to your hearing preferences, providing you with the most accurate and enjoyable sound.

Hearing Health: The AirPods Pro 2 come with features that promote better hearing health, including the ability to track and manage your hearing exposure. With features like hearing protection and notifications when your listening volume is too high, the AirPods Pro 2 help safeguard your hearing over time.

Why They Are Considered a Top-Tier Audio Accessory for iPhone Users

The AirPods Pro 2 stand out not only because of their advanced features but also because they are fully integrated into the Apple ecosystem. This makes them a top-tier audio accessory for iPhone users for several reasons:

Seamless Integration with Apple Devices: The AirPods Pro 2 work effortlessly with all Apple devices, including iPhone, iPad, Mac, Apple Watch, and Apple TV. Pairing is quick and simple, thanks to the H2 chip, which enhances connectivity and ensures that the AirPods Pro 2 automatically switch between devices without any hassle. For example, you can seamlessly switch from listening to music on your iPhone to watching a movie on your iPad or attending a Zoom call on your MacBook.

Apple-Specific Features: The AirPods Pro 2 support Apple-specific features like Siri voice control, the ability to adjust volume with a swipe on the stem, and automatic switching between devices. These features add to the convenience and make the AirPods Pro 2 an essential accessory for anyone deeply embedded in the Apple ecosystem.

Compatibility with Apple's Health and Fitness Features: The AirPods Pro 2 are compatible with Apple Health, allowing you to track your hearing health over time. This integration extends to the fitness features on the Apple Watch, where the AirPods Pro 2 can be used to enhance your workout experience with personalized audio cues.

What's New in the AirPods Pro 2?

Apple has made several notable improvements in the AirPods Pro 2, not only in terms of sound quality and features but also in terms of design and performance. Here's an overview of the key enhancements:

Enhancements in Sound Quality, Design, and Performance

Sound Quality: The introduction of the new H2 chip brings a significant boost in sound quality. The H2 chip enables better noise cancellation and clearer sound, with improved bass and more detailed high frequencies. The custom-built drivers and amplifiers in the AirPods Pro 2 provide richer audio and more balanced sound across all types of content, whether you're listening to music, watching movies, or making calls.

Design Improvements: The AirPods Pro 2 have a more refined design, offering a more secure fit with the inclusion of new silicone ear tips in four sizes. The design has been optimized to be more comfortable, particularly during extended listening sessions. The charging case has also been updated with a built-in speaker that helps you locate it if you misplace it, and it's now equipped with a lanyard loop for added portability.

Battery Life: The battery life of the AirPods Pro 2 has been extended, allowing for up to six hours of listening time with ANC activated. The charging case adds even more battery life, giving you up to 30 hours of use. The case also supports MagSafe charging, allowing for convenient wireless charging.

Introduction of the H2 Chip and What It Means for Users

The most significant upgrade in the AirPods Pro 2 is the introduction of the H2 chip. This chip is responsible for powering many of the advanced features of the AirPods Pro 2, including:

Improved Sound Quality: The H2 chip optimizes the sound processing for richer, more dynamic audio. It enhances the listening experience by delivering better bass, more accurate highs, and overall more detailed sound.

Enhanced Active Noise Cancellation: With the new H2 chip, the AirPods Pro 2 offer up to twice the noise cancellation performance of the first-generation model. This means that you can block out even more ambient noise, providing an even more immersive listening experience.

Better Connectivity: The H2 chip ensures that the AirPods Pro 2 maintain a stable and fast connection to your Apple devices, with reduced latency and quicker switching between devices.

CHAPTER 1

Getting Started with Your AirPods Pro 2
Unboxing and First Impressions

Unboxing a new product is always an exciting experience, and the Apple AirPods Pro 2 are no exception. From the moment you open the box, Apple's attention to detail is evident. The packaging is sleek, simple, and designed to make the unboxing process as delightful as possible. Let's take a closer look at what you can expect when you open the box and explore each item in detail.

A Detailed Look at the Packaging and Contents

Apple has maintained its signature minimalistic design for the AirPods Pro 2 packaging. The box is clean, featuring a picture of the AirPods Pro 2 on the front. Upon lifting the top flap, the first thing you'll see is the AirPods Pro 2 themselves neatly nestled in their charging case. The earbuds are carefully positioned in a foam insert, ensuring that they remain protected during transit and storage.

The charging case is compact and has a matte finish, distinguishing it from previous models. This case, which also serves as a key feature of the AirPods Pro 2, is equipped with a speaker to help you locate it using the Find My app, as well as a lanyard loop for easier portability.

Underneath the foam insert, you'll find a few essential accessories:

Silicone Ear Tips: The AirPods Pro 2 come with four sizes of silicone ear tips (XS, S, M, L). These ensure a comfortable and secure fit for different ear shapes and sizes, improving both sound quality and noise isolation.

Lightning to USB-C Cable: Apple includes a cable for charging the case. This cable is also used for wired connections, making it easy to charge your case through a USB-C port.

Documentation: A quick start guide, warranty information, and Apple's regulatory information are tucked into a small compartment. The guide offers helpful tips on setting up and using your AirPods Pro 2.

While the contents of the box are simple, Apple ensures that everything included is practical and useful. There's no unnecessary packaging, and everything is neatly organized, reflecting Apple's commitment to high-quality design.

Introduction to the AirPods, Charging Case, and Accessories

The AirPods Pro 2 are compact, sleek, and comfortable. Each earbud features a polished white design with a small stem. The design has been optimized to fit securely in the ear while also providing comfort for long listening sessions. The ear tips, as mentioned earlier, are available in four sizes to help users find the most comfortable fit. Proper ear tip sizing is crucial to achieving the best sound quality and noise cancellation, so it's important to experiment with different sizes to find the one that fits best for you.

The charging case is slightly larger than the previous model but still compact enough to easily slip into your pocket or bag. It features a glossy finish with a built-in speaker for locating it using the Find My app. The case is also equipped with a lanyard loop, offering an extra level of convenience when you need to carry the case around. Another new feature of the charging case is that it supports both wireless and wired charging, making it versatile for different charging setups.

As for the accessories, the silicone ear tips are soft and flexible, designed to mold to the shape of your ear canal for a snug fit. They are an essential part of getting the best performance out of the AirPods Pro 2, as they help ensure proper sound isolation and comfort.

How to Handle the AirPods Pro 2 with Care Right Out of the Box

When handling the AirPods Pro 2 for the first time, it's essential to treat them with care to ensure they remain in optimal condition. Here are a few tips for handling your new AirPods:

Avoid Excessive Force: The AirPods Pro 2 are lightweight and delicate, so avoid pressing or bending the stems unnecessarily. They are designed for comfort, and any rough handling may damage the internal components.

Properly Store the AirPods: Always place the AirPods back into their charging case when not in use. This protects them from dirt, dust, and potential damage. The case is also equipped with a magnet that helps secure the AirPods in place, preventing them from rattling around.

Clean the AirPods Pro 2 Regularly: While the AirPods themselves are resistant to sweat and water (IP54 rating), they still require regular cleaning to prevent earwax build-up. Use a soft, dry cloth to wipe down the exterior, and if necessary, use a gentle brush to clean the mesh of the earbud.

Store the Case in a Safe Place: The charging case is the most vulnerable part of the AirPods Pro 2, as it contains the charging mechanism. Be mindful of where you place it to prevent scratches or dents. Using a case cover or sleeve can help protect the case from everyday wear and tear.

By following these care tips, you'll keep your AirPods Pro 2 in great condition for a long time.

Initial Setup and Pairing with Apple Devices

Once you've unboxed your AirPods Pro 2 and are ready to begin using them, the next step is to set them up and pair them with your Apple devices. Pairing the AirPods Pro 2 is a simple and intuitive process, and in just a few steps, you can have your new earbuds connected to your iPhone, iPad, or Mac.

Step-by-Step Guide on Pairing Your AirPods Pro 2 with iPhone, iPad, or Mac

Pairing with iPhone:

Open the Charging Case: With the AirPods Pro 2 inside their charging case, open the lid to start the pairing process. This automatically activates the pairing mode.

Bring the Case Near Your iPhone: Hold the open charging case near your unlocked iPhone. A setup prompt should appear on the screen, showing an image of the AirPods Pro 2.

Tap "Connect": Once the setup prompt appears, tap the "Connect" button on your iPhone's screen. The AirPods Pro 2 will automatically pair with your device.

Finish Setup: If this is your first time using AirPods Pro 2, you may be prompted to set up features like "Hey Siri" and Personalized Spatial Audio. Follow the on-screen instructions to complete the setup.

Ready to Use: Once the setup is complete, you're ready to start using your AirPods Pro 2. You can now enjoy music, take calls, and use Siri with ease.

Pairing with iPad:

The process for pairing with an iPad is similar to that of an iPhone. Open the case near the iPad, and the setup prompt will appear. Tap "Connect" to complete the pairing process.

Pairing with Mac:

Open Bluetooth Preferences on Your Mac: Click the Apple menu at the top-left corner of the screen and select "System Preferences." Then, click on "Bluetooth."

Open the Charging Case: Open the lid of the charging case with the AirPods Pro 2 inside. The AirPods should appear in the Bluetooth menu on your Mac.

Click "Connect": Click the "Connect" button next to the AirPods Pro 2 in the Bluetooth preferences window.

Done: Your AirPods Pro 2 are now connected to your Mac. You can start using them for audio, video calls, or other activities.

Bluetooth Pairing Instructions and Tips for Troubleshooting

Bluetooth pairing is typically straightforward, but if you encounter any issues, here are some troubleshooting tips:

Ensure Bluetooth is Enabled: Check that Bluetooth is turned on in the settings of your iPhone, iPad, or Mac. If Bluetooth is off, your device won't be able to detect the AirPods.

Reset the AirPods Pro 2: If you're unable to pair your AirPods Pro 2 with your device, try resetting them. To do this, press and hold the button on the back of the case until the status light flashes amber, then white. This resets the connection and allows you to pair the AirPods again.

Update Your Device's Software: Ensure that your device's software is up-to-date. Apple frequently releases updates that can improve Bluetooth connectivity and overall functionality.

Check for Interference: If there are many Bluetooth devices in your vicinity, it may cause interference. Try pairing your AirPods Pro 2 in a less crowded area.

Unpair and Re-pair: If the AirPods Pro 2 are paired with another device, unpair them from that device first before attempting to pair with a new one.

Exploring the AirPods Pro 2 Features via the 'Find My' App

One of the standout features of the AirPods Pro 2 is the ability to locate them using Apple's Find My app. This is especially useful if you misplace the charging case or the earbuds themselves. The AirPods Pro 2 have several features that make this process even easier.

How to Locate Your AirPods Using the Find My Feature

To use Find My to locate your AirPods Pro 2:

Open the Find My App: Open the Find My app on your iPhone, iPad, or Mac. If you don't have the app, you can download it from the App Store.

Select Your AirPods Pro 2: In the app, select the "Devices" tab, and you should see your AirPods Pro 2 listed. Tap on your AirPods in the list.

Play a Sound: If your AirPods are nearby, tap the "Play Sound" button. Your AirPods will emit a chime to help you locate them, even if they are buried under a pile of clothes or hidden in another room.

Locate the Charging Case: If you've misplaced the charging case, it's also trackable. The Find My app will show you the last known location of the case on a map, helping you pinpoint where you last left it.

Use Precision Finding (iPhone 11 and Later): If you have an iPhone 11 or later, you can use Precision Finding. This feature uses the Ultra-Wideband (UWB) chip to give you step-by-step directions to your AirPods Pro 2, similar to using an augmented reality system.

How the Find My Feature is Enhanced in the Pro 2

The AirPods Pro 2 offer enhanced features when it comes to locating them. The new charging case is equipped with a built-in speaker, which allows the case to emit a sound when prompted through the Find My app. This makes it much easier to find the case, even if it's hidden under a couch or in a drawer.

Additionally, with the inclusion of the speaker, the AirPods Pro 2's location is even more precise, and you can track them down much faster compared to the first generation. The AirPods themselves can also be located with higher accuracy, ensuring that you never lose them for too long.

CHAPTER 2

Understanding the Key Features of AirPods Pro 2

The Apple AirPods Pro 2 are packed with innovative features designed to provide an unmatched audio experience, whether you're listening to music, taking calls, or watching movies. The seamless integration of cutting-edge technology with user-centric design has made the AirPods Pro 2 a standout in the world of wireless earbuds. In this chapter, we will delve into the core features that set the AirPods Pro 2 apart, including Active Noise Cancellation (ANC), Transparency Mode, Spatial Audio, Personalized Sound, and how to achieve a customizable fit for maximum comfort.

Active Noise Cancellation (ANC) and Transparency Mode

One of the defining features of the AirPods Pro 2 is their advanced Active Noise Cancellation (ANC) technology. Whether you're commuting, working in a noisy office, or simply seeking peace and quiet, ANC has revolutionized how we experience sound.

What ANC Does and How to Toggle It On/Off

Active Noise Cancellation works by using external microphones to detect ambient sounds, such as the hum of an airplane engine or chatter from a nearby conversation. Once detected, the AirPods Pro 2 generate sound waves that are the exact inverse (anti-phase) of the surrounding noise. These opposing sound waves effectively cancel out the unwanted noise, providing you with a more immersive and quiet listening experience.

To toggle ANC on or off, follow these steps:

Using the AirPods Pro 2:

Ensure the AirPods Pro 2 are properly inserted into your ears.

Press and hold the stem of either earbud to switch between Active Noise Cancellation (ANC) and Transparency Mode.

Using the Control Center on iPhone:

Open the **Control Center** on your iPhone by swiping down from the top-right corner (on Face ID models) or up from the bottom (on models with a home button).

Press and hold the **volume slider** to bring up the AirPods Pro 2 options.

Toggle between **Noise Cancellation** and **Transparency** based on your needs.

You can also adjust ANC and Transparency Mode settings in the **Settings app** under **Bluetooth** by selecting your AirPods Pro 2 and customizing the settings to your preference.

How Transparency Mode Works and When to Use It for Situational Awareness

While ANC is designed to block out the noise around you, Transparency Mode offers the opposite effect. When activated, Transparency Mode lets you hear the world around you without removing your AirPods. This is particularly helpful when you need to stay aware of your surroundings, such as when crossing a busy street, talking to someone, or needing to hear an announcement at an airport.

When Transparency Mode is activated, the AirPods Pro 2 use external microphones to capture the ambient sounds and then play them into your ears along with your audio. The result is a natural listening experience where you can still hear your music or podcasts, while also remaining aware of the environment around you.

Situational Uses of Transparency Mode:

In Public Spaces: When you're walking through a city, traveling on public transport, or shopping, Transparency Mode ensures you can hear important sounds like traffic or conversations while still enjoying your audio.

During Conversations: Transparency Mode allows you to continue listening to your music while still being able to engage in a conversation without needing to remove your earbuds.

When Exercising Outdoors: If you're jogging or cycling, Transparency Mode allows you to hear oncoming traffic or pedestrians, enhancing safety while you work out.

Tips for Optimizing Noise Cancellation During Flights, Public Spaces, and at Home

Active Noise Cancellation is particularly useful in environments with consistent, low-frequency noise, such as airplanes, buses, and crowded areas. Here are some tips for optimizing ANC for different scenarios:

During Flights:

Airplanes often generate a constant, low-pitched hum, which is perfect for ANC technology to block out. Set your AirPods Pro 2 to ANC mode and enjoy a peaceful flight.

For long-haul flights, it's important to periodically check the fit of your AirPods to ensure they are sealed in your ears, as this maximizes the noise-cancelling effects.

In Public Spaces:

Public spaces can have a mix of random sounds, like chatter, footsteps, and background noise. For maximum noise reduction, ensure your AirPods Pro 2 are snug in your ears, and activate ANC to block out distractions.

When sitting in a noisy café or library, ANC helps you focus on your work or reading by eliminating the sound of nearby conversations and music.

At Home:

At home, ANC can help you create a focused, quiet space, whether you're working, studying, or simply relaxing. The AirPods Pro 2 work well to filter out household noise like TV sounds, conversations, and appliance hums.

Spatial Audio and Personalized Sound

One of the most exciting features of the AirPods Pro 2 is **Spatial Audio**, which takes the listening experience to the next level by providing a more immersive sound. By using advanced algorithms and head tracking, Spatial Audio brings a surround sound effect to your earbuds, simulating a more natural and expansive audio experience. This is a game-changer for media consumption, allowing you to feel more connected to the content you're experiencing.

How Spatial Audio Enhances the Listening Experience

Spatial Audio works by simulating a three-dimensional audio environment around you. Instead of the sound coming from just the left and right channels like traditional stereo audio, Spatial Audio positions sounds around you in a 360-degree space. This creates a more immersive and dynamic experience, especially for watching movies, playing games, or listening to music that has been mixed with this technology.

For example, when watching a movie on your iPhone or iPad, Spatial Audio ensures that sounds seem to come from the direction of the action on screen. If a character moves across the screen, the sound will shift accordingly, creating a realistic audio experience. This level of immersion is especially useful when using AirPods Pro 2 with Dolby Atmos-supported content, such as movies and music available on platforms like Apple TV+ and Apple Music.

Spatial Audio also helps enhance music listening by providing a more open soundstage. With the right setup, you'll feel like you're sitting in the middle of a concert, with the sound enveloping you from all angles.

Setting Up and Customizing Personalized Spatial Audio

Personalized Spatial Audio takes this experience a step further by tailoring the surround sound to your specific hearing needs. Using the **TrueDepth camera** on your iPhone, you can create a profile of your ears and head shape. This profile ensures that the sound is customized to fit your unique anatomy, optimizing the audio for a truly personalized experience.

Setting Up Personalized Spatial Audio:

Open the Settings App: On your iPhone, navigate to **Settings > Bluetooth**.

Select Your AirPods Pro 2: Tap the "i" next to your AirPods Pro 2 in the device list.

Personalized Spatial Audio: You will see an option for **Personalized Spatial Audio**. Tap to start the setup process.

Use the TrueDepth Camera: Follow the on-screen instructions to scan your face and ears using the front-facing camera on your iPhone.

Enjoy the Experience: After setting up, Spatial Audio will be automatically personalized for you when you listen to supported content.

Why Dynamic Head Tracking is a Game Changer for Media Consumption

One of the key features that truly distinguishes Spatial Audio in the AirPods Pro 2 is **Dynamic Head Tracking**. This technology allows the sound to move with your head, so you experience audio from the correct position, regardless of how you turn or tilt your head.

For example, if you're watching a movie and you turn your head to the side, the audio will adjust accordingly, making it feel as though the sound is coming from the direction of the screen. This makes watching movies and TV shows feel much more like a traditional surround sound system, but in the convenience of your wireless earbuds.

Head tracking also works with music, where it can provide a more dynamic and immersive listening experience. Whether you're listening to an orchestral piece or a rock concert, Dynamic Head Tracking adjusts the sound to match your head movements, creating a sense of space and depth that you can't get from regular headphones.

Customizable Fit for Maximum Comfort

A good fit is essential for ensuring both the best audio experience and effective noise cancellation with your AirPods Pro 2. Apple has gone to great lengths to ensure that the AirPods Pro 2 provide a customizable and comfortable fit for all users, allowing for longer listening sessions without discomfort.

Importance of Ear Tip Size for Better Sound and Noise Cancellation

The silicone ear tips that come with the AirPods Pro 2 play a crucial role in delivering optimal sound and noise isolation. If the ear tips are too small or too large, they can negatively affect the sound quality and the effectiveness of Active Noise Cancellation. A proper seal ensures that external noise is blocked out, and that the sound is delivered clearly into your ears without interference.

Choosing the right ear tip size depends on the shape of your ear canal. Apple provides four sizes (XS, S, M, L), which gives you the flexibility to find the one that fits you best. In general:

If the ear tips are too small, you may feel a lack of noise isolation and the bass response will likely be weak.

If the ear tips are too large, they may feel uncomfortable and could cause sound distortion.

A well-fitting ear tip provides better sound quality, more effective ANC, and more comfort.

How to Use the Fit Test Feature to Find the Best Ear Tip Size

Apple has integrated a **Fit Test** feature in the AirPods Pro 2 that allows you to ensure you're using the correct ear tip size for a perfect seal. Here's how to use it:

Insert the AirPods Pro 2 into your ears: Choose the ear tips that feel most comfortable and insert the AirPods Pro 2.

Open Settings on Your iPhone: Go to **Settings > Bluetooth**, then tap the "i" next to your AirPods Pro 2.

Run the Fit Test: Under **Ear Tip Fit Test**, select **Play Test**. The AirPods will play a short sound and analyze the fit. The test will let you know if you're using the right ear tip size.

Adjust if Necessary: If the test suggests a better fit, swap out the ear tips for the recommended size and retake the test.

Maintaining Comfort During Long Listening Sessions

Comfort is key, especially if you plan to wear your AirPods Pro 2 for extended periods. To ensure maximum comfort:

Choose the Right Fit: As mentioned earlier, the Fit Test feature helps you find the right ear tip size. A good seal not only improves sound quality and ANC but also prevents discomfort.

Take Breaks: Even with a good fit, it's important to take occasional breaks to rest your ears during long listening sessions.

Use the Right Placement: Make sure the AirPods are inserted properly and that the stems are not too tight against your ear. This ensures both comfort and optimal performance.

The AirPods Pro 2 are packed with features designed to enhance the listening experience, from Active Noise Cancellation and Transparency Mode to Personalized Spatial Audio and Dynamic Head Tracking. With customizable fit options, the AirPods Pro 2 ensure maximum comfort and performance, no matter how long you wear them. Whether you're looking for noise isolation during travel, immersive sound for media consumption, or a secure fit for your daily routine, the AirPods Pro 2 deliver on every front, making them a top-tier choice for anyone looking for high-quality wireless earbuds.

CHAPTER 3

Managing Battery Life and Charging for AirPods Pro 2

The Apple AirPods Pro 2 are not just about exceptional sound quality and performance, but also about how effectively they manage power. Battery life is a key factor for any wireless audio device, and Apple has taken strides to ensure that the AirPods Pro 2 offer impressive usage time while incorporating advanced charging capabilities. In this chapter, we'll explore the battery life for the AirPods Pro 2 and their charging case, how to monitor and manage battery usage, and practical tips for conserving battery life.

Battery Life for the AirPods Pro 2 and Charging Case

One of the standout features of the AirPods Pro 2 is their battery life. Apple has managed to significantly improve the power efficiency of the AirPods while still packing in the high-end features that make them so desirable. Battery life can make or break the user experience, and Apple's optimization of this aspect makes the AirPods Pro 2 a reliable companion for daily use.

Overview of Listening Time, Talk Time, and Total Usage with the Case

Listening Time:

With Active Noise Cancellation (ANC) turned on, the AirPods Pro 2 offer up to **6 hours** of listening time on a single charge. If you're someone who listens to music during workouts, commutes, or while relaxing at home, this 6-hour window provides plenty of time before needing to recharge.

When **ANC** is turned off, you can enjoy up to **7 hours** of listening time. This slight increase in battery life when ANC is not in use is due to the lower power consumption without the constant noise-cancelling process running.

Talk Time:

For calls, the AirPods Pro 2 provide up to **4.5 hours** of talk time with a single charge. This is especially useful for those who rely on their earbuds for conference calls, work-related communications, or social calls. The sound quality during calls is crystal clear, thanks to the adaptive beamforming microphones that isolate your voice from ambient noise.

Total Usage with the Charging Case:
The AirPods Pro 2 come with a compact and portable charging case that offers multiple charges to keep you going. With the case, you can achieve a total of up to **30**

hours of listening time with ANC enabled. The charging case itself holds enough power to recharge the earbuds about 4-5 times, depending on how often you use ANC and the volume at which you listen.

The case itself has a larger battery compared to previous models, which allows the AirPods Pro 2 to support long periods of use, making them ideal for long trips or extended sessions of use without access to a charging point.

Charging the AirPods Pro 2

Charging the AirPods Pro 2 is a seamless process, made even more convenient with multiple options for power. Whether you prefer using traditional methods like a wired connection or more modern solutions like wireless charging, Apple has provided flexible options to suit a variety of needs.

How to Charge the AirPods Using the Case (MagSafe, Lightning, or Wireless Charging)

The AirPods Pro 2 come with a charging case that can be charged in three different ways:

MagSafe Charging:

MagSafe charging is one of the most convenient methods, as it allows you to place the case on a MagSafe charger, which uses magnets to align the case perfectly with the charging pad. Simply place the case on the MagSafe charger, and it will begin charging. The magnet helps to ensure that the charging case is positioned correctly to receive power without needing to align the ports manually.

Charging Status: A small LED indicator on the front of the case shows the status of the charge. If the light is green, the case is fully charged; if it's amber, it still needs charging.

Lightning Cable:

For those who prefer wired charging, you can charge the AirPods Pro 2's case via the **Lightning port**. Using the included Lightning to USB-C cable, plug one end into the charging case and the other end into a compatible charging block, such as an Apple power adapter, or any USB port.

This method allows for consistent and reliable charging without worrying about wireless connections, and it's also faster than wireless charging, depending on the power brick used.

Wireless Charging:

The case supports **Qi wireless charging**, which means you can use any Qi-compatible wireless charging pad to charge the AirPods case. Simply place the charging case with the AirPods inside it on a wireless charging pad, and charging will begin automatically. This is one of the easiest methods, as there are no cables involved, and it can be more convenient in various environments, like on your nightstand or desk.

Charging Status: As with MagSafe, the LED indicator will show the charging status.

How to Charge the Case Itself and When to Do It

Charging the case is just as easy as charging the AirPods. Since the case holds enough power to recharge the AirPods multiple times, it is essential to keep the case charged, especially for users who rely on it for extended listening sessions.

Charging the Case:

The case can be charged through the **Lightning port** or using **MagSafe** or **Qi wireless charging**, as previously mentioned.

Charging Frequency: Ideally, you should charge the case once its charge drops below 25% to ensure it's always ready to provide power to the AirPods when needed. Since the AirPods can last up to 6-7 hours on a single charge, most users will need to charge the case once or twice a week, depending on usage.

When to Charge the Case:

Before Low Power Alert: When the AirPods case reaches around 25% or lower in battery, you'll likely receive a notification on your paired iPhone or other Apple devices. Charging the case before it's completely drained will help keep it in good condition and ready for use.

Regular Charging: If you're a frequent user who relies on the AirPods for calls, music, and other activities, charging the case overnight (or when not in use) ensures that it remains fully charged, so the AirPods are always ready to go.

Battery Conservation Tips

Even with the impressive battery life of the AirPods Pro 2, managing how you use them and following certain practices can help extend their lifespan and optimize their overall efficiency. These tips are designed to help you get the most out of your AirPods, ensuring they last longer and stay in top condition.

Best Practices to Prolong Battery Life

Turn Off ANC When Not Needed:
Active Noise Cancellation (ANC) is a powerful feature that requires battery power to operate. While ANC is invaluable in noisy environments, you can save battery by turning it off when it's not necessary, such as when you're in a quiet room or at home. To toggle ANC, simply press and hold the stem of your AirPods Pro 2 or adjust the settings in the Control Center of your iPhone.

Use Transparency Mode Sparingly:
Similar to ANC, **Transparency Mode** uses the external microphones to pick up surrounding sounds. While useful, it also consumes more battery than listening in passive mode. If you're in a quiet environment, it's

advisable to turn off Transparency Mode to conserve battery life.

Lower the Volume:

Listening at high volumes can quickly drain your battery. Try to maintain a moderate volume when listening to music or podcasts. High volumes not only use more battery but can also affect the sound quality. Lowering the volume can significantly extend battery life.

Turn Off 'Hey Siri' Feature:

If you're not using Siri frequently, turning off the **"Hey Siri"** feature can save power. This setting listens for your voice at all times, and although it's useful for hands-free control, it can drain the battery if left on unnecessarily.

Use One Earbud at a Time:

For those who don't need full stereo sound, using just one earbud at a time can extend battery life. The AirPods Pro 2 are designed to work in mono mode, so you can still take calls or listen to music with a single earbud while preserving battery.

How to Manage Settings to Optimize Battery Usage

Apple provides several settings that can help optimize battery performance and conserve energy. Here's how to manage them:

Optimize Battery Charging:

The AirPods Pro 2 come with an **Optimize Battery Charging** feature, which is designed to slow the rate of battery aging by learning your charging routine. This feature uses machine learning to understand when you typically charge your AirPods and will only charge the battery to 80% until it's closer to the time you usually unplug the device. To enable this feature, go to **Settings > Bluetooth** on your iPhone, tap the "i" next to your AirPods, and enable **Optimized Battery Charging**.

Use Low Power Mode (On iPhone):

When your iPhone's battery is running low, switching to **Low Power Mode** can also help conserve battery on your AirPods. This feature limits background processes and reduces power consumption across your Apple devices. You can activate Low Power Mode by going to **Settings > Battery** and toggling it on.

Turn Off Automatic Switching:

If you don't need your AirPods Pro 2 to automatically switch between devices, you can turn off this feature to save battery. You can disable this by going to **Settings > Bluetooth**, selecting your AirPods, and toggling off **Automatic Switching**.

Avoid Extreme Temperatures:
Temperature extremes can reduce the lifespan of your AirPods Pro 2's battery. Avoid exposing them to excessive heat or cold for prolonged periods. Storing them at room temperature ensures optimal battery health.

The Apple AirPods Pro 2 offer impressive battery life and charging flexibility, providing up to 6-7 hours of listening time on a single charge and a total of 30 hours with the charging case. With multiple charging options—MagSafe, Lightning, and wireless charging—the AirPods Pro 2 cater to various preferences and use cases. By following battery conservation tips and managing settings effectively, users can maximize the lifespan and performance of their AirPods, ensuring that they continue to deliver outstanding audio quality for years to come. Whether you're on the go, at home, or traveling, these earbuds provide the power and convenience you need.

CHAPTER 4

Advanced Features and Customizations for AirPods Pro 2

The Apple AirPods Pro 2 are more than just high-quality earbuds; they are a powerhouse of advanced features designed to integrate seamlessly into your daily life. These features go beyond just listening to music and making calls, offering a level of control, customization, and connectivity that sets the AirPods Pro 2 apart from other wireless audio devices. In this chapter, we'll explore Siri integration, automatic switching between Apple devices, and the touch controls that provide users with a highly customizable and intuitive experience.

Siri Integration and Voice Commands

Siri, Apple's voice-activated virtual assistant, has been a hallmark of the Apple ecosystem for years, and the AirPods Pro 2 integrate it seamlessly for hands-free control. Whether you're on the go, working out, or just relaxing at home, Siri allows you to interact with your AirPods without ever needing to lift a finger. This is particularly valuable when you're busy or need to keep your hands free for other tasks.

How to Use Siri with AirPods Pro 2 for Hands-Free Control

To use Siri with your AirPods Pro 2, all you need to do is activate the voice assistant using the phrase **"Hey Siri."** Once you've set up Siri on your iPhone or other Apple device, your AirPods Pro 2 can automatically connect to Siri through their built-in microphones, allowing you to issue voice commands while your hands remain free.

Activate Siri Using Your Voice:

Simply say, **"Hey Siri"** followed by your request. You don't need to touch your AirPods, and you can use Siri to perform tasks like adjusting the volume, playing music, sending texts, setting reminders, or checking the weather.

Siri is always listening for the "Hey Siri" command, so there's no need to press any buttons or interact physically with your AirPods Pro 2. This hands-free functionality is incredibly useful for multitasking, exercising, or driving.

Activate Siri Using the Stem:

If you don't want to use the voice trigger, you can **activate Siri** by **pressing and holding the stem** of either earbud. Once you hear the chime, you can then ask Siri to perform your desired action, such as making a call or controlling your media.

Using Siri for Basic Functions:

Play Music or Podcasts: Simply say, "Hey Siri, play my playlist" or "Hey Siri, play my podcast."

Adjust Volume: You can also adjust the volume with Siri, saying commands like, "Hey Siri, turn the volume up" or "Hey Siri, lower the volume."

Answer Calls: If you're on a call and need to answer or hang up, you can say, "Hey Siri, answer the call" or "Hey Siri, end the call."

Send Texts and Set Reminders: You can dictate texts or set reminders, such as, "Hey Siri, send a text to John" or "Hey Siri, remind me to call Mom at 3 p.m."

Get Directions or Weather Updates: Ask for driving directions or weather forecasts, e.g., "Hey Siri, give me directions to the nearest coffee shop" or "Hey Siri, what's the weather like today?"

Common Commands and Tips for Efficient Use

To get the most out of Siri, it's helpful to understand the range of commands that work well with the AirPods Pro 2. Here are some of the most commonly used commands and tips for efficient voice control:

General Commands:

"Hey Siri, play some music."

"Hey Siri, pause the music."

"Hey Siri, skip to the next track."

"Hey Siri, stop the music."

Device Control:

"Hey Siri, turn off noise cancellation."

"Hey Siri, turn on transparency mode."

"Hey Siri, adjust the volume."

Communication:

"Hey Siri, call [contact name]."

"Hey Siri, send a message to [contact name]."

"Hey Siri, read my unread messages."

Smart Home and Utilities:

"Hey Siri, turn off the lights."

"Hey Siri, set the thermostat to 72 degrees."

"Hey Siri, open the garage door."

Tips for Efficient Use:

Use Specific Commands: While Siri is powerful, it's best to be specific with your commands. For example, instead of saying "Play music," say "Play my workout playlist."

Customize Siri Settings: You can fine-tune Siri's settings to match your preferences. Go to **Settings > Siri & Search** to adjust options like voice feedback, language, and whether Siri listens for the "Hey Siri" command.

Voice Feedback for Headphones: For an improved experience, enable **Announce Notifications** under **Settings > Notifications** to have Siri read incoming notifications aloud through your AirPods Pro 2.

Automatic Switching Between Devices

One of the standout features of the AirPods Pro 2 is **automatic switching** between devices in the Apple ecosystem. This feature makes it easier than ever to move between your iPhone, iPad, Mac, or Apple Watch without needing to manually connect your AirPods to each device.

Explanation of the Handoff Feature Across Apple Devices

Automatic switching is powered by the **Handoff** feature, a hallmark of the Apple ecosystem that allows for seamless transitions between Apple devices. For example, you might be listening to music on your iPhone, and then switch to watching a movie on your MacBook. With automatic switching, your AirPods Pro 2 will seamlessly move from one device to the next, ensuring that you don't have to pause or reconnect your earbuds.

Here's how Handoff works:

Using iCloud for Device Synchronization:
The AirPods Pro 2 use **iCloud** to sync across all of your Apple devices. This allows your AirPods to connect to the device you're actively using, automatically switching based on the device's needs. Whether you're listening to music on your iPhone or participating in a

video call on your Mac, the AirPods Pro 2 always know which device to connect to.

Seamless Device Transitions:

For example, if you're listening to music on your iPhone and you start watching a YouTube video on your Mac, your AirPods Pro 2 will automatically switch to the Mac. Similarly, if you get a call while watching a movie on your iPad, your AirPods will immediately switch to the iPhone, allowing you to answer the call seamlessly.

No Manual Intervention Needed:

The beauty of this feature is that it works without you needing to do anything. Once your AirPods are paired with your Apple devices, they will automatically switch based on which device is playing audio. You no longer have to manually disconnect and reconnect your AirPods, making it easier than ever to manage multiple devices.

How to Switch Seamlessly from iPhone to iPad or Mac Without Manual Intervention

Switching between devices is incredibly simple, as it's done automatically through the AirPods Pro 2's

51

integration with your iCloud account and Apple's ecosystem. Here's how to ensure everything is set up for smooth switching:

Ensure All Devices are Using the Same Apple ID:
For the automatic switching feature to work, all of your Apple devices must be signed into the same Apple ID. This ensures that your AirPods can be synchronized across devices through iCloud.

Keep Devices Nearby and Active:
Make sure that your devices are turned on and within Bluetooth range. If your AirPods Pro 2 are connected to an active device, they will prioritize the active device's audio. For instance, if you're listening to music on your iPhone and start a video on your iPad, your AirPods will automatically switch to the iPad.

Using Your AirPods for Audio on Multiple Devices:
If you're switching from an iPhone to a Mac, just start playing audio on your Mac. Your AirPods will automatically detect the switch and begin playing audio through the Mac. The same applies when transitioning from an iPad to your iPhone or Apple Watch.

Check the Bluetooth Settings if Needed: If automatic switching doesn't seem to work, check the Bluetooth settings on your devices. Go to **Settings > Bluetooth** on your iPhone or iPad, select your AirPods Pro 2, and ensure that **Automatic Switching** is enabled under the device options. You can also manually select the AirPods for a specific device if automatic switching isn't working properly.

Touch Controls and Customization

The AirPods Pro 2 are equipped with intuitive **touch controls** that allow users to adjust volume, skip tracks, and answer calls with ease. These controls are located on the stems of the AirPods, providing an effortless way to manage your audio without reaching for your phone.

How to Adjust Volume, Skip Tracks, and Answer Calls Using the Touch Sensors

The AirPods Pro 2's touch-sensitive stems make controlling your music or calls simple and intuitive. Here's a breakdown of how to use the touch controls:

Adjusting Volume:

Volume Up/Down: To adjust the volume, swipe up or down on the **stem** of the AirPods Pro 2. A quick swipe will increase or decrease the volume slightly, while a long swipe will make larger adjustments.

Note: This feature works only with the AirPods Pro 2, as the previous generation didn't include volume controls.

Skipping Tracks:

Skip Forward: To skip to the next track, **double-tap** the stem of either earbud.

Skip Back: To go back to the previous track, **triple-tap** the stem. This is especially helpful if you want to replay a song or move to the next one in your playlist.

Answering Calls:

Answering a Call: To answer an incoming call, **press the stem once**. The call will automatically route to your AirPods, and you can begin talking hands-free.

Ending a Call: To end a call, simply **press the stem once** again.

Declining a Call: If you want to decline a call, **double-tap** the stem.

How to Customize Touch Control Settings in the AirPods Pro 2 Settings

Apple provides a level of customization for the touch controls on the AirPods Pro 2, allowing you to adjust the functionality to fit your preferences.

Access the Settings:

Open the **Settings app** on your iPhone and navigate to **Bluetooth**. Find your AirPods Pro 2 in the list of devices and tap the **"i"** next to the device name.

Customize Controls:

Under the **Press and Hold** section, you'll find the options for customizing the touch controls.

You can choose whether to use the **Press and Hold** action for switching between ANC and Transparency Mode, or whether you'd like it to activate Siri instead.

You can also modify double-tap and triple-tap functions for skipping tracks or answering calls.

Adjust Touch Sensitivity:

If you find that the touch controls are too sensitive or not responsive enough, there is an option in the settings to adjust the sensitivity of the touch controls. This ensures a more comfortable and personalized experience.

The AirPods Pro 2 are packed with advanced features that make them stand out in the world of wireless earbuds. Siri integration, automatic device switching, and customizable touch controls offer a level of flexibility and ease of use that enhances the overall experience. By using voice commands, switching seamlessly between Apple devices, and taking full advantage of the touch-sensitive controls, you can tailor your AirPods Pro 2 to fit your needs perfectly. These features combine to make the AirPods Pro 2 not just a pair of earbuds, but a fully integrated part of the Apple ecosystem, designed to make your life more convenient and enjoyable.

CHAPTER 5

Exploring the Health Features of AirPods Pro 2

The AirPods Pro 2 are not just advanced wireless earbuds that offer exceptional sound quality and seamless connectivity within the Apple ecosystem; they also come equipped with a range of health-related features designed to enhance your well-being. From monitoring hearing health to providing noise exposure alerts, the AirPods Pro 2 offer a variety of tools that can help protect your hearing and integrate into your broader health and fitness goals. In this chapter, we will explore these health-focused features in-depth, discussing how they work and how you can use them to maintain better hearing and overall wellness.

Hearing Health and Protection

One of the most significant aspects of the AirPods Pro 2 is their focus on **hearing health**. Apple has been working toward creating products that not only deliver superior sound but also safeguard users' hearing over time. The AirPods Pro 2 are equipped with features that provide valuable insights into your hearing health and actively work to prevent damage from prolonged exposure to loud sounds.

How AirPods Pro 2 Can Help Monitor Hearing Health

Apple has incorporated several technologies into the AirPods Pro 2 to help users monitor and protect their hearing health. These features are designed to alert users to potential risks and encourage safer listening habits.

Hearing Health Monitoring: AirPods Pro 2 integrate with the **Apple Health app** to track your audio exposure. The AirPods track the sound levels in your environment, as well as the volume at which you're listening to music or other audio. This allows the Apple Health app to monitor how much time you're exposed to potentially harmful sound levels throughout the day.

Tracking Audio Exposure: With AirPods Pro 2, you can view **how long you've been exposed to sound levels above 80 decibels (dB)**, which is the threshold at which prolonged exposure can begin to damage hearing. The Apple Health app will show you a record of this exposure, including data such as when and how often your volume exceeded recommended levels.

Hearing Health Notifications: In addition to tracking exposure, AirPods Pro 2 offer notifications that let you know if you're at risk of hearing damage. When the listening volume exceeds safe levels for extended periods, you'll receive a warning on your iPhone, prompting you to reduce the volume.

Sound Recognition: In addition to helping users manage their volume levels, AirPods Pro 2 are equipped with sound recognition features. Using advanced machine learning, the AirPods Pro 2 can recognize certain environmental sounds—such as sirens or alarms—and alert you when they are present in your surroundings. This feature can contribute to better situational awareness and safety, particularly when you're out walking or jogging in a busy city.

The Importance of Using the Hearing Aid Function for Users with Hearing Impairments

For individuals with hearing impairments, the AirPods Pro 2 also provide an essential **Hearing Aid function**, which offers a more accessible and effective way to amplify sound. This feature, which is available through the **Live Listen** function in the iOS settings, essentially turns the AirPods into a hearing aid by amplifying external sounds.

Live Listen Function: The **Live Listen** function enables users to use their iPhone as a microphone to amplify sound and send it directly to their AirPods Pro 2. This can be particularly helpful for individuals who have difficulty hearing conversations in noisy environments or in one-on-one interactions. The microphone on the iPhone picks up ambient sounds, and the AirPods Pro 2 deliver the amplified sounds directly to the user's ears, providing more clarity and better understanding.

How to Activate Live Listen:

Open **Settings** on your iPhone.

Navigate to **Control Center** and tap the **Customize Controls** option.

Add the **Hearing** option to the Control Center.

Once added, you can open the Control Center on your iPhone and tap the **Hearing icon** to enable **Live Listen**.

Adjust the sensitivity of the microphone to enhance the volume of sounds you want to hear.

This feature can significantly improve the quality of life for those with hearing loss, providing them with an affordable and discreet alternative to traditional hearing aids.

Customizing Audio Settings for Hearing Loss: For users who have specific hearing loss in certain frequencies, the AirPods Pro 2 offer custom audio settings that help tailor the sound profile. This can be done through the **Personalized Audio** feature in the AirPods settings on your iPhone, where the device uses your iPhone's TrueDepth camera to create a personalized listening experience.

How to Set Up Personalized Audio for Hearing Loss:

Open **Settings > Bluetooth**, then tap the "i" next to your AirPods Pro 2.

Select **Audio Accessibility Settings**.

Enable **Custom Audio Setup**, and follow the on-screen instructions to adjust the audio output based on your hearing preferences.

These settings allow users to boost certain frequencies where they may have hearing deficits, improving the clarity of speech and everyday sounds.

Noise Exposure Alerts

Long-term exposure to loud environments can have a detrimental impact on your hearing. AirPods Pro 2 are designed to help you avoid damage by providing real-time **noise exposure alerts**. These alerts are part of Apple's commitment to promoting safer listening habits and preventing hearing damage from excessive noise exposure.

How AirPods Notify You About Prolonged Exposure to Loud Environments

The AirPods Pro 2's **noise exposure alerts** function by monitoring the intensity of the sounds around you and providing notifications when the volume levels exceed safe limits. For example, if you're listening to music at high volumes in a noisy environment, the AirPods Pro 2 will track the sound exposure and alert you when it reaches harmful levels.

The 80/80 Rule: Apple recommends following the **80/80 rule** for safe listening: Keep the volume at or below 80% of the maximum volume and limit your listening time to no more than 80 minutes per day at high volumes. If you listen to audio above 80 decibels (dB) for extended periods, you risk damaging your hearing.

Exposure Notifications: If you listen to music or other audio content at high volumes for an extended period, the AirPods Pro 2 will send a notification to your device, warning you about the potential risk. This proactive approach helps users be more aware of their listening habits and make adjustments before damage occurs.

Adjusting Notifications in the Settings: You can adjust how these notifications work by navigating to **Settings > Sounds & Haptics** on your iPhone. Under the **Headphone Safety** section, you can customize the thresholds for exposure alerts, allowing you to choose when and how you want to receive notifications about your listening habits.

Tips on Adjusting Volume to Avoid Hearing Damage

To preserve your hearing, it's important to adopt healthy listening habits and make adjustments to your AirPods Pro 2's settings. Here are some tips to help you manage volume levels and avoid damage:

Lower the Volume: The easiest way to protect your hearing is by keeping the volume at a reasonable level. The AirPods Pro 2 allow you to adjust the volume via **touch controls**, Siri, or the volume slider on your iPhone. Avoid cranking the volume up to maximum levels, especially in noisy environments.

Use Noise Cancellation:

To enjoy better sound quality at lower volumes, use the **Active Noise Cancellation (ANC)** feature. By blocking out external sounds, ANC lets you enjoy your music or podcasts without the need for high volume levels.

Take Breaks:

Regularly give your ears a break from listening to loud audio. Try the **60/60 rule**—keep your volume at 60% of maximum and listen for no more than 60 minutes at a time. If you're listening to audio for long periods, take regular breaks to reduce the risk of hearing damage.

Monitor Audio Exposure in the Health App: The Apple Health app allows you to track your weekly audio exposure, so you can keep a close eye on how much time you've spent listening at high volumes. This data can help you stay informed about your listening habits and make necessary adjustments.

Using AirPods Pro 2 as a Health Tool

The AirPods Pro 2 aren't just about music and calls—they also fit into **Apple's larger health ecosystem**, where they play an important role in fitness tracking and overall well-being. By integrating seamlessly with the **Apple Health app**, your AirPods Pro 2 can track more than just your audio exposure—they can become part of a holistic approach to health, fitness, and wellness.

How AirPods Pro 2 Fits into Apple's Larger Health Ecosystem (Apple Health App)

Apple has designed a cohesive **health ecosystem** that includes the **Apple Watch**, **iPhone**, and now the AirPods Pro 2, allowing users to monitor various aspects of their well-being. Through the **Apple Health app**, data collected from your AirPods Pro 2 can be combined with data from other Apple devices to give a comprehensive overview of your health.

Tracking Physical Activity: Although the AirPods themselves are not fitness trackers, they integrate with your **Apple Watch** and **iPhone** to provide data on your activity. For example, if you're using your AirPods Pro 2 during a workout, you can track your calories burned, distance covered, and heart rate on the Apple Health app.

Hearing Health Insights: The integration of hearing data into the Health app gives you a visual overview of your **audio exposure** over time. This can be particularly useful for those who want to monitor their listening habits and ensure they are staying within safe limits.

Apple Fitness+ Integration: If you subscribe to **Apple Fitness+**, your AirPods Pro 2 can enhance the experience by delivering real-time audio cues during workouts. For instance, when participating in a running or cycling workout, you can receive spoken instructions and feedback, helping you stay motivated and on track.

Insights into Using AirPods Pro 2 for Fitness Tracking and Well-Being

While the AirPods Pro 2 do not directly track physical metrics like heart rate or steps, they play a supportive role in fitness tracking and wellness. Here's how you can make the most of your AirPods Pro 2 for fitness and overall health:

Listening to Guided Workouts:
Use your AirPods Pro 2 to listen to **guided workouts** from the Apple Fitness+ app. These audio-based workouts can help you focus on form, technique, and motivation, making your fitness routine more effective and enjoyable.

Mindfulness and Meditation:

The AirPods Pro 2's **Adaptive Transparency** feature is particularly useful for mindfulness and meditation sessions. By blocking out external distractions while allowing you to hear calming sounds or guided meditation sessions, the AirPods Pro 2 provide a focused, peaceful experience.

Tracking Active Listening Time:

In the Health app, your listening habits are tracked as part of your overall wellness data. By monitoring how much time you spend listening to audio, you can assess whether you're maintaining a balanced lifestyle that includes both audio exposure and physical activity.

The AirPods Pro 2 offer a robust suite of **health-related features** that go beyond entertainment and communication. With tools to monitor hearing health, alert you about harmful noise exposure, and integrate seamlessly into Apple's health ecosystem, these earbuds provide a comprehensive approach to maintaining and improving your well-being. Whether you're using the Hearing Aid function to assist with hearing loss, receiving notifications about excessive noise exposure, or tracking your audio habits alongside fitness data in the

Health app, the AirPods Pro 2 are a powerful health tool. By incorporating these features into your daily routine, you can protect your hearing, optimize your wellness, and stay more connected to your overall health goals.

CHAPTER 6

Troubleshooting and Care for AirPods Pro 2

The Apple AirPods Pro 2 is a sophisticated piece of technology that blends advanced features with seamless integration into the Apple ecosystem. However, like all electronic devices, they are not immune to occasional issues. Whether it's a pairing problem, connectivity issue, or difficulty with charging, understanding how to troubleshoot these common problems can help you resolve them quickly and get the most out of your AirPods Pro 2. Additionally, proper maintenance and cleaning are essential to ensuring the longevity and optimal performance of your AirPods Pro 2. This chapter will cover troubleshooting common issues, cleaning and maintaining your AirPods, and how to restore your AirPods to factory settings when necessary.

Common Issues and How to Fix Them

While the AirPods Pro 2 are generally reliable, you may encounter a few common issues such as pairing problems, connectivity disruptions, or sound quality concerns. Below, we'll go over these issues and how to resolve them, ensuring that your AirPods Pro 2 are functioning at their best.

Pairing Problems and How to Fix Them

AirPods Pro 2 are designed to pair effortlessly with your Apple devices, but sometimes issues can arise, preventing a smooth connection. Here's how to address pairing problems:

Ensure Bluetooth is Enabled:
The first step in troubleshooting pairing issues is ensuring that Bluetooth is enabled on your device. Go to **Settings > Bluetooth** on your iPhone, iPad, or Mac, and check if Bluetooth is turned on.

Make Sure AirPods are in Pairing Mode:
For the AirPods Pro 2 to enter pairing mode, the charging case must be open with the AirPods inside. If the AirPods do not automatically go into pairing mode, you can press and hold the setup button on the back of the charging case until the status light begins blinking white. This indicates that the AirPods are ready to pair.

Forget and Reconnect AirPods:
If the AirPods are having trouble pairing with a specific device, try **forgetting** the AirPods in your Bluetooth settings and then reconnecting them. To do this, go to **Settings > Bluetooth**, tap the "i" next to your AirPods,

and select **Forget This Device**. Then, follow the pairing steps again to reconnect your AirPods.

Check for Interference or Distance Issues: Bluetooth performance can be affected by interference or range. Ensure there are no physical obstructions between your AirPods and the paired device. If there are many Bluetooth devices around, try moving to a quieter space to avoid interference.

Restart the Device:

Sometimes, a simple restart of the device you are pairing with can resolve connectivity issues. Turn off the Bluetooth and restart your iPhone, iPad, or Mac, then try pairing the AirPods again.

Reset Your AirPods:

If none of the above steps work, you can reset your AirPods Pro 2 to factory settings, which may resolve pairing issues. Instructions for this are provided later in this chapter.

Connectivity Issues and How to Fix Them

If your AirPods Pro 2 are paired but not connecting properly, or if you experience intermittent sound drops, the following steps can help restore connectivity:

Check the Battery:

If the battery on your AirPods or charging case is low, it could cause connectivity issues. Ensure your AirPods Pro 2 are charged by placing them in the case and checking the battery levels on your paired device (iPhone, iPad, etc.). You can also check the charge level by opening the charging case near your iPhone.

Re-pair with Bluetooth Settings:

As with pairing problems, one solution for connectivity issues is to disconnect and reconnect your AirPods via the Bluetooth settings. Go to **Settings > Bluetooth**, find your AirPods, and tap the "i" next to them. Then tap **Disconnect** or **Forget This Device** and follow the pairing steps again.

Reset Network Settings on Your Device:

If connectivity issues persist, try resetting the network settings on your iPhone or iPad. This will clear any problematic connections and reset Bluetooth settings to their default. To reset the network settings, go to **Settings > General > Reset > Reset Network Settings**. Note that this will also reset Wi-Fi and other network-related settings, so you may need to reconnect to your networks afterward.

Disable Automatic Switching Temporarily: The AirPods Pro 2 automatically switch between Apple devices when they are in range. While this feature is convenient, it can sometimes cause connectivity issues. Temporarily disabling automatic switching can help, which can be done by going to **Settings > Bluetooth**, selecting your AirPods, and toggling off **Connect to This iPhone**.

Sound Quality Concerns and How to Fix Them

If you notice distorted audio, muffled sound, or low volume, it can be frustrating, but there are ways to troubleshoot sound quality problems with your AirPods Pro 2.

Check the Fit and Seal:
A poor seal can affect sound quality, particularly the bass response. Make sure the AirPods are inserted properly in your ears and that the silicone tips are the correct size for your ears. If the fit feels loose, try adjusting the ear tips or switching to a different size to create a better seal.

Turn Off ANC or Transparency Mode (If Necessary):

73

If you're using Active Noise Cancellation (ANC) or Transparency Mode, the settings could impact the sound quality depending on the environment. ANC, while excellent at blocking out external noise, can sometimes distort the sound if the seal isn't perfect. Try turning off ANC to see if that improves sound quality.

Adjust Audio Balance Settings:

Sometimes, uneven sound can be caused by audio balance settings. On your iPhone or iPad, go to **Settings > Accessibility > Audio/Visual** and make sure the audio balance is set to the center. This ensures that the sound is balanced between both earbuds.

Reset the AirPods:

If all else fails and you continue to experience sound issues, a reset may fix the problem. The instructions for resetting your AirPods are provided later in this chapter.

What to Do When the AirPods Are Not Charging or Not Turning On

If your AirPods Pro 2 won't charge or turn on, this could be due to several issues, including battery problems or a faulty charging case. Here's what you can do:

Ensure the Charging Case Is Charged: First, check the charging case's battery. Open the case and look at the status light. If the light is off, the case may not have power, or there may be an issue with the charging cable. Try charging the case with a Lightning cable or wireless charger for at least 30 minutes to ensure it has enough power.

Clean the Charging Port and Connectors: Dirt or debris in the charging port or on the AirPods' charging connectors can prevent them from charging properly. Use a soft, dry cloth or a small, soft brush to gently clean the charging contacts inside the case. Ensure that both the charging case and the AirPods are free from any buildup that could prevent proper contact.

Try a Different Charging Cable or Charger: If your AirPods are still not charging, try using a different Lightning cable or wireless charger to rule out issues with the charging equipment. Ensure the cable is properly connected to the charging case.

Reset the AirPods:
If your AirPods won't turn on, even after confirming that they are charged, it may help to reset them. Press and hold the setup button on the back of the case for

about 15 seconds, until the status light flashes amber and then white, indicating that the AirPods have been reset.

Cleaning and Maintaining AirPods Pro 2

Regular cleaning and maintenance of your AirPods Pro 2 ensure they continue to perform optimally and last longer. Proper care can prevent issues like poor sound quality, uncomfortable fit, and even physical damage. Let's look at how to clean your AirPods Pro 2 without damaging them, the products you can use, and tips for keeping them in top condition.

How to Clean the Earbuds and Case Without Damaging Them

Cleaning your AirPods Pro 2 correctly is essential to avoid any potential damage to their sensitive components. Follow these steps to clean the earbuds and charging case safely:

Cleaning the AirPods:

Use a Soft Cloth: To clean the exterior of the AirPods, use a soft, lint-free cloth. Lightly dampen the cloth with water if needed, but avoid using any harsh chemicals or abrasives.

Clean the Mesh Microphones and Speakers: For the mesh microphones and speakers, use a soft brush (like a small paintbrush or toothbrush) to gently remove any dirt or debris. Avoid pressing hard, as this could damage the mesh.

Avoid Water Exposure: The AirPods Pro 2 are water-resistant but not fully waterproof. Avoid submerging them in water or exposing them to excessive moisture. If they get wet, wipe them with a dry cloth and allow them to air dry completely before using them again.

Cleaning the Charging Case:

Exterior Cleaning: Use a soft, dry cloth to wipe the exterior of the charging case. You can slightly dampen the cloth if necessary, but avoid getting moisture inside the case.

Clean the Charging Ports: Use a dry cotton swab or a soft brush to gently clean the charging port and the area around it. Dirt or debris in the charging port can interfere with the charging process.

What Products to Use for Safe Cleaning

When cleaning your AirPods Pro 2, always use non-abrasive materials to avoid scratching or damaging the surface. Here are the best products to use for cleaning:

Microfiber Cloth: Soft, lint-free microfiber cloths are ideal for cleaning the exterior of your AirPods and case. They will remove dust, fingerprints, and smudges without causing damage.

Cotton Swabs: For cleaning small areas like the charging port or the mesh on the AirPods, a dry cotton swab is an effective and safe tool.

Soft-Bristled Brush: A soft brush, such as a small paintbrush or a toothbrush, can be used to clean delicate areas like the speaker and microphone meshes.

Tips for Preventing Earwax Buildup and Keeping the Charging Port Clean

Use the Right Ear Tips: Using the correct size of ear tips will help prevent earwax buildup and improve sound quality. The AirPods Pro 2 come with several ear tip sizes, so experiment to find the one that fits best.

Regular Cleaning: Clean your AirPods and their ear tips regularly to prevent earwax buildup. Remove the ear tips from the AirPods, rinse them with water (if necessary), and gently wipe them with a soft cloth.

Store AirPods in the Charging Case: Always store your AirPods in their case when not in use. This prevents dust, dirt, and moisture from accumulating on the earbuds and ensures that they remain safe and clean.

Restoring the AirPods to Factory Settings

If you've tried troubleshooting and cleaning your AirPods Pro 2 and are still facing issues, restoring them to factory settings may help. This process resets all settings and removes any pairing information, which can resolve persistent issues.

When and Why to Reset Your AirPods Pro 2

You may need to reset your AirPods Pro 2 in the following situations:

Persistent Pairing Issues: If your AirPods are not connecting to your device properly, resetting them may clear any configuration problems.

Connectivity Problems: When the AirPods are not switching devices as expected or having trouble maintaining a connection, a reset can help resolve these issues.

Restoring Default Settings: If you want to remove your AirPods from your Apple ID or reset them before giving them away or selling them, resetting is necessary.

Step-by-Step Instructions for Resetting and Re-pairing

Place the AirPods in the Charging Case: Ensure both AirPods are inside the case, and the lid is open.

Press and Hold the Setup Button: On the back of the charging case, press and hold the small setup button for about 15 seconds. The status light on the front of the case will flash amber, indicating that the AirPods are resetting.

Reconnect to Your Devices: Once the AirPods are reset, the status light will flash white, signaling that they are in pairing mode. You can now pair the AirPods with your device again by following the standard pairing procedure.

Proper troubleshooting, cleaning, and resetting are essential for ensuring that your AirPods Pro 2 continue to deliver optimal performance. By following these guidelines for fixing common issues, maintaining the cleanliness of your earbuds and case, and resetting your AirPods when necessary, you can maximize their lifespan and enjoy a consistent, high-quality audio experience. Regular care and timely troubleshooting will ensure that your AirPods Pro 2 remain a reliable and effective accessory for years to come.

CHAPTER 7

Accessory Guide for AirPods Pro 2

Apple's AirPods Pro 2 are sophisticated earbuds that provide an exceptional listening experience, thanks to their active noise cancellation, sound quality, and seamless integration with the Apple ecosystem. However, to enhance the usability, portability, comfort, and protection of your AirPods Pro 2, there are a variety of accessories designed specifically for them. Additionally, while AirPods Pro 2 work best within the Apple ecosystem, they can also be paired with non-Apple devices. In this chapter, we will explore the best accessories for your AirPods Pro 2 and explain how to use them with non-Apple devices, covering both the advantages and limitations.

Choosing the Right Accessories for Your AirPods Pro 2

AirPods Pro 2 are a premium product, and the right accessories can enhance their functionality and ensure they remain in good condition over time. Whether you're looking for protection, additional comfort, or ways to maximize portability, there are several accessories available to make the most of your AirPods Pro 2.

Protective Cases, Ear Tips, and Other Add-Ons to Enhance Usability

One of the most important considerations when purchasing accessories for your AirPods Pro 2 is protection. The earbuds and their charging case are compact and sleek but also prone to scratches, dents, or damage if dropped. Below are some of the top accessories to protect your AirPods and enhance their overall usability:

Protective Cases for the Charging Case: The AirPods Pro 2 charging case, while durable, can get scratched and damaged over time. Protective cases can provide an extra layer of security, preventing wear and tear. These cases come in a variety of materials, colors, and designs.

Silicone Cases: Silicone cases are the most popular choice for AirPods Pro 2 protection. They are soft, flexible, and provide a great grip, preventing the case from slipping out of your hands. Additionally, they cushion the case in case of accidental drops. Silicone cases are available in a wide range of colors and often include a keychain loop, making it easy to attach the case to your bag or belt.

Leather Cases: For those who prefer a more premium look and feel, leather cases offer a stylish and luxurious option. Leather cases provide a more refined appearance while still offering protection against scratches and bumps. However, they tend to be less grippy than silicone cases, so you may want to be careful when handling them.

Hard Shell Cases: For maximum protection, hard shell cases are an excellent option. These cases offer sturdier protection against drops and impacts. Some hard shell cases even come with a clip, allowing you to easily attach your AirPods case to your bag or backpack. Although these cases provide solid protection, they may add some bulk to the overall design.

Ear Tips: One of the most important features of the AirPods Pro 2 is the customizable fit, which is provided by the interchangeable silicone ear tips. Having the right fit is crucial for both comfort and sound quality, as a poor seal can lead to discomfort and degraded noise cancellation performance.

Choosing the Right Ear Tip Size: Apple provides the AirPods Pro 2 with three sizes of silicone ear tips: small, medium, and large. For the best fit, it's important to experiment with each size to find the one that fits comfortably in your ear canal. Apple also offers an **Ear Tip Fit Test**, which is available in the Bluetooth settings of your paired device. This test ensures that you're using the correct ear tip size for an optimal seal.

Third-Party Ear Tips: If you find that the included ear tips are uncomfortable or don't create a proper seal, third-party manufacturers offer alternative ear tips that may better suit your needs. Many of these are made from soft foam or memory foam, which can provide a more secure and comfortable fit for some users. Additionally, foam tips can enhance the noise cancellation properties of the AirPods Pro 2, providing a better overall listening experience.

Wireless Charging Pads: The AirPods Pro 2 charging case supports **MagSafe** and **Qi wireless charging**, which means you can charge the case without needing to plug in a cable. A wireless charging pad is an essential accessory if you prefer a cable-free charging experience. Many wireless charging pads are compatible with both MagSafe and Qi devices, allowing you to place the case on the pad for an effortless charging experience.

MagSafe-Compatible Charging Pads: MagSafe charging pads are specifically designed to work seamlessly with AirPods Pro 2. These pads use magnets to align your charging case precisely with the charging coils, ensuring an efficient charge. Some MagSafe chargers also offer **fast charging**, allowing you to get a quick top-up when you're on the go.

Portable Wireless Chargers: If you need to charge your AirPods Pro 2 while traveling, portable wireless chargers are a great option. These compact, battery-powered charging pads allow you to charge your AirPods Pro 2 case on the go, eliminating the need for a power outlet.

Keychains and Clips: To make carrying your AirPods Pro 2 more convenient, you can opt for keychains or clips designed specifically for the AirPods Pro 2 case. These accessories make it easy to attach the case to your bag, backpack, or belt loop, ensuring you always have your AirPods with you and easily accessible.

Keychain Cases: Many silicone and leather protective cases come with a built-in keychain loop, so you can easily attach your AirPods case to your keys or bag.

Carabiner Clips: Some protective cases also come with a **carabiner clip**, which allows you to attach your AirPods case to your backpack, purse, or belt loop. This is especially useful for people who are always on the go and need quick access to their AirPods.

Cleaning Kits: Keeping your AirPods Pro 2 clean is essential for maintaining sound quality and comfort. Over time, earwax, dirt, and debris can accumulate in the earbuds and charging case, leading to poor performance or discomfort. A **cleaning kit** designed for AirPods can help you safely clean the earbuds without damaging them. These kits typically include tools like microfiber cloths, cleaning brushes, and cleaning wipes that are gentle on delicate electronics.

How to Use the AirPods Pro 2 with Non-Apple Devices

While the AirPods Pro 2 are optimized for use within the Apple ecosystem, they are also compatible with **non-Apple Bluetooth devices**. Whether you're using Android phones, Windows PCs, or other Bluetooth-enabled devices, you can still enjoy all of the core features of the AirPods Pro 2, such as sound quality, noise cancellation, and the ability to take calls. However, there are some limitations and differences in the experience when using the AirPods Pro 2 with non-Apple products. Below, we will discuss how to pair your AirPods with Android phones and non-Apple devices, as well as some of the limitations that come with using them outside the Apple ecosystem.

Pairing with Android Phones and Non-Apple Bluetooth Devices

Pairing the AirPods Pro 2 with Android phones or other non-Apple Bluetooth devices is a straightforward process. Since the AirPods Pro 2 use Bluetooth for connectivity, they will work with any device that supports Bluetooth audio.

Step-by-Step Guide to Pairing with an Android Phone:

Open the AirPods Pro 2 Case: With your AirPods Pro 2 inside the case, open the lid to activate pairing mode.

Activate Bluetooth on Your Android Device: Go to **Settings > Bluetooth** on your Android phone and ensure that Bluetooth is turned on.

Find Your AirPods Pro 2: After opening the case, you should see the AirPods Pro 2 appear in the list of

88

available devices in the Bluetooth menu on your Android phone.

Tap to Pair: Tap on the AirPods Pro 2 in the Bluetooth menu to initiate pairing. The AirPods Pro 2 should connect within a few seconds, and you'll be ready to use them.

Pairing with Windows PCs and Other Bluetooth Devices:

Activate Bluetooth on Your PC or Device: Ensure Bluetooth is enabled on your Windows PC or Bluetooth-enabled device. On Windows 10 or 11, go to **Settings > Devices > Bluetooth & Other Devices** and turn on Bluetooth.

Open the Charging Case: As with Android devices, open the AirPods Pro 2 case to enter pairing mode.

Select AirPods Pro 2 on Your Device: Look for your AirPods in the Bluetooth device list and click to pair.

Limitations and Differences in Experience When Using AirPods with Non-Apple Products

While the AirPods Pro 2 are fully compatible with Android phones and other Bluetooth devices, there are several key differences in the experience when using them outside of the Apple ecosystem. Below are some of the limitations:

No Seamless Switching Between Devices: One of the standout features of the AirPods Pro 2 within the Apple ecosystem is their ability to **automatically switch** between Apple devices. For example, you can seamlessly switch between listening to music on your iPhone and taking a call on your MacBook without manually reconnecting. This feature is not available when using the AirPods with non-Apple devices, so you will need to manually disconnect and reconnect your AirPods if you want to switch between devices.

Limited Access to Advanced Features: Some of the more advanced features of the AirPods Pro 2, such as **Personalized Spatial Audio** and **Siri integration**, are not fully supported on non-Apple devices. While you can still use the basic functions like music playback, calls, and ANC, features like **Adaptive Transparency**, **Spatial Audio**, and **Siri** require an Apple device to function optimally.

Lack of Automatic Device Switching: As mentioned earlier, automatic switching between Apple devices is not supported when using the AirPods Pro 2 with non-Apple products. You will need to manually disconnect from one device and reconnect to another if you wish to switch between devices.

Limited Customization of Controls: On Apple devices, you can customize the **touch controls** of the AirPods Pro 2 for functions such as volume control, skipping tracks, and activating Siri. This level of customization is generally not available when using the AirPods with Android phones or other Bluetooth devices.

Choosing the right accessories for your AirPods Pro 2 can significantly enhance your experience, providing protection, comfort, and convenience. Protective cases, ear tips, wireless chargers, and cleaning kits are all essential accessories that can help extend the life of your AirPods and improve their performance. Additionally, while the AirPods Pro 2 are optimized for use with Apple products, they are also fully compatible with non-Apple Bluetooth devices. However, the experience may not be as seamless, and some advanced features may be limited when used with Android phones or Windows PCs. Understanding these differences and selecting the appropriate accessories will ensure that your AirPods Pro 2 serve you well, no matter the device they're paired with.

CHAPTER 8

Getting the Most Out of Your AirPods Pro 2

The AirPods Pro 2 offer an array of powerful features designed to enhance your listening experience, making them a versatile and essential accessory for anyone within the Apple ecosystem. From maximizing sound quality to creating a custom listening experience and seamlessly integrating with other Apple devices, the AirPods Pro 2 are packed with possibilities. In this chapter, we will explore how to get the most out of your AirPods Pro 2 by optimizing sound quality, customizing your listening experience, and leveraging the full potential of the Apple ecosystem.

Maximizing Sound Quality and Listening Experience

One of the most significant aspects of the AirPods Pro 2 is their ability to deliver exceptional sound quality, thanks to their advanced hardware and software integration. Whether you're listening to music, watching a movie, or taking a call, the AirPods Pro 2 offer a sound experience that is both rich and immersive. However, to truly maximize sound quality, it's essential to adjust a few settings and understand the best environments for specific features like Spatial Audio and Active Noise Cancellation (ANC).

Adjusting Settings for Personalized Listening Preferences

AirPods Pro 2 come with several customizable features designed to enhance your sound experience. Adjusting these settings according to your preferences can make a significant difference in the overall listening experience.

Personalized Spatial Audio: Personalized Spatial Audio is one of the standout features of the AirPods Pro 2, providing a 3D sound experience that makes you feel as though the sound is coming from all around you. By using the **TrueDepth camera** on your iPhone, you can create a personalized listening profile that tailors the sound based on the shape and size of your ears and head.

How to Set Up Personalized Spatial Audio:

Open the **Settings** app on your iPhone.

Navigate to **Bluetooth** and select your AirPods Pro 2 from the list of devices.

Under the **Spatial Audio** section, select **Personalized Spatial Audio**.

Follow the on-screen instructions to scan your head and ears with the TrueDepth camera.

Once set up, this feature ensures that sound is accurately positioned around you, adjusting dynamically based on your head movements for an immersive experience that feels natural and lifelike.

Adaptive Transparency: Adaptive Transparency mode adjusts the amount of external sound you hear based on your surroundings. It amplifies important sounds like voices and traffic, making it ideal for busy environments, while still maintaining a level of isolation from the noise around you.

How to Adjust Transparency Mode:

You can toggle **Transparency Mode** by pressing and holding the stem of your AirPods Pro 2.

Alternatively, you can access the **Control Center** on your iPhone and adjust the transparency level to suit your preferences.

Active Noise Cancellation (ANC): ANC is a powerful feature that eliminates unwanted external sounds, making it perfect for situations where you need focus and peace, such as on a plane or in a crowded café. You can activate ANC by pressing and holding the stem of your AirPods or by adjusting the settings through your iPhone.

How to Adjust ANC Settings:

Open **Settings** > **Bluetooth**, then select your AirPods Pro 2.

In the settings menu, toggle **Noise Cancellation** or **Transparency** as needed.

Additionally, AirPods Pro 2 features an **adaptive ANC** mode that adjusts the noise cancellation level based on your surroundings, giving you a more tailored experience.

The Best Genres and Environments for Spatial Audio and ANC

Maximizing sound quality involves not only adjusting the settings but also understanding the best genres and environments for using certain features. Here's how you can get the most out of **Spatial Audio** and **ANC** for different situations:

Spatial Audio with Music:

Best Genres: Spatial Audio works best with genres that have complex soundscapes and dynamic elements, such as **classical**, **orchestral**, **cinematic scores**, or **electronic music**. These genres benefit from the immersive 3D sound that Spatial Audio provides, allowing you to hear instruments and sounds positioned all around you.

Best Environments: For the best experience, use Spatial Audio in quiet environments where you can sit back and enjoy music without distractions. Using Spatial Audio on your iPhone, iPad, or MacBook while watching movies or listening to music on platforms that support Dolby Atmos also enhances the experience.

ANC with Music:

Best Genres: ANC is particularly effective for genres that require clear sound and no distractions. **Classical**, **jazz**, and **ambient music** are ideal for ANC because the clarity and detail of these genres shine when external noises are blocked out.

Best Environments: ANC is most effective in noisy environments like airplanes, public transport, and crowded cafes. It's perfect for when you need to focus and block out ambient noise while listening to your favourite tunes.

ANC with Movies or Podcasts:

ANC can also enhance the experience of watching movies or listening to podcasts by isolating you from surrounding distractions. For cinematic audio experiences, turn on ANC and Spatial Audio together to create a dynamic, surround-sound effect that draws you into the content.

Creating a Custom Listening Experience

AirPods Pro 2 offers several ways to personalize your audio experience, from adjusting equalizer settings to customizing sound profiles for clearer calls. These features ensure that you get the most out of your listening sessions, whether you're enjoying music, watching movies, or taking calls.

How to Use Equalizer Settings and Custom Presets for Optimal Sound

The AirPods Pro 2 offer users the ability to customize their sound profiles for an optimal audio experience. Apple's **Music app** provides built-in equalizer (EQ) settings, allowing you to fine-tune the bass, treble, and mid-range frequencies for different genres or personal preferences.

Adjusting EQ Settings on iPhone:

Go to **Settings** > **Music** > **EQ** on your iPhone.

Select from a list of preset EQ settings, including options like **Bass Booster**, **Treble Booster**, and **Loudness**.

For a more customized experience, you can adjust the EQ settings to your liking. For example, if you prefer deeper bass or clearer highs, use the appropriate preset.

Using Third-Party Apps for Custom Sound Profiles: For even more control over your listening experience, consider using third-party audio apps like **Boom** or **AudioFi**. These apps allow you to create custom EQ presets and store them for easy access, offering finer control over your sound profile. You can save different presets for different types of music, allowing you to quickly switch between settings.

Enhancing Call Quality for Clearer Conversations

The AirPods Pro 2 are equipped with advanced microphone technology that enhances call quality, ensuring that your conversations come through loud and clear. Here's how you can optimize call quality:

Using the Beamforming Microphone: The AirPods Pro 2 use **adaptive beamforming microphones** that focus on your voice while blocking out background noise. This ensures that your voice is clear during calls, even in noisy environments.

Enabling the "Voice Isolation" Mode: Apple's latest software updates have introduced a feature called **Voice Isolation**, which uses machine learning to prioritize your voice and minimize background noise during calls. To enable this feature, make sure your AirPods Pro 2 are connected to your device, and use the **Control Center** to select the **Voice Isolation** option.

Use ANC during Calls in Noisy Environments: ANC can also be used during phone calls, especially in noisy environments. This allows you to block out unwanted noise and focus on the conversation. Just press and hold the stem to activate ANC during calls.

Exploring the Ecosystem: AirPods Pro 2 with Apple Watch, iPad, and More

One of the greatest advantages of the AirPods Pro 2 is their seamless integration with the Apple ecosystem. Whether you're using your AirPods with an Apple Watch, iPad, or Mac, you can enjoy a unified experience that makes switching between devices effortless.

Integrating AirPods with Other Apple Products for a Unified Experience

AirPods Pro 2 are designed to work seamlessly with all Apple products, from iPhones and Macs to Apple Watches and iPads. This integration creates a fluid, connected experience that allows you to move between devices without interruption.

AirPods with iPhone and iPad:

Seamless Pairing: AirPods Pro 2 automatically connect to your iPhone or iPad as long as you're signed in with the same Apple ID. When you open the AirPods case near your device, it will recognize them and connect instantly.

Automatic Switching: If you're listening to music on your iPhone and start watching a video on your iPad, your AirPods Pro 2 will automatically switch to the iPad without you needing to do anything. This automatic switching is powered by **iCloud** and works across all Apple devices.

AirPods with Apple Watch:

Music and Fitness Tracking: When you pair your AirPods Pro 2 with your Apple Watch, you can listen to music or podcasts directly from the watch without needing to carry your phone. This is perfect for workouts or runs when you want to leave your phone behind. The watch also allows you to control your AirPods' settings (volume, skip tracks, etc.) directly from the watch.

Fitness + Integration: If you subscribe to **Apple Fitness+**, you can use your AirPods Pro 2 to listen to workout instructions or watch guided fitness videos. The integration with the **Apple Health app** also allows you to track your fitness data while enjoying your workouts.

AirPods with Mac:

Handoff for Calls and Audio: If you're listening to music or podcasts on your iPhone and want to continue on your Mac, your AirPods Pro 2 will automatically switch to your Mac once you start playing audio. This handoff feature allows you to seamlessly continue your activity across devices.

FaceTime Calls and Video Conferencing: AirPods Pro 2 are excellent for FaceTime calls and video conferencing on your Mac. The built-in microphones deliver clear voice audio, and the adaptive noise cancellation ensures that background noise is minimized, making for better call quality.

How to Use Your AirPods Pro 2 for More Than Just Music

AirPods Pro 2 are more than just a tool for listening to music. With integration into the Apple ecosystem, your AirPods can be used for various other purposes that enhance productivity, entertainment, and communication.

Using AirPods Pro 2 with Apple TV:

Immersive Audio for Movies and TV Shows: AirPods Pro 2 can be connected to your Apple TV to deliver an immersive audio experience for movies and TV shows. When watching content that supports Dolby Atmos or surround sound, you'll feel as if the sound is coming from all around you, thanks to **Spatial Audio**.

Private Listening: For those who prefer private listening, AirPods Pro 2 allow you to enjoy TV shows and movies without disturbing others. Whether you're watching a late-night show or enjoying a movie, the AirPods Pro 2 provide clear, high-quality audio without any distractions.

Podcasts and Audiobooks:

Comfortable Listening for Extended Periods: AirPods Pro 2 are perfect for long listening sessions, whether you're enjoying your favourite podcast or audiobook. The comfortable fit and active noise cancellation ensure you can focus on the content without distractions. Use Siri to skip to the next episode or pause your podcast hands-free.

FaceTime Calls and Video Calls:

Hands-Free Communication: Use your AirPods Pro 2 to make FaceTime calls, participate in video calls, or hold business meetings. The clear sound quality and excellent microphone performance ensure that your voice is heard loud and clear. ANC also helps filter out background noise, making it easier for you to hear the other person.

The AirPods Pro 2 are a premium accessory that offers more than just exceptional sound. With customizable sound settings, seamless integration with the Apple ecosystem, and powerful features like Spatial Audio and ANC, you can tailor your listening experience to suit any environment. Whether you're using your AirPods Pro 2 for music, movies, calls, or fitness, these earbuds provide a versatile and immersive experience that enhances your daily life. By maximizing sound quality, creating a custom listening experience, and leveraging the power of the Apple ecosystem, you can ensure that your AirPods Pro 2 continue to meet your needs, no matter what you use them for.

CONCLUSION

AirPods Pro 2

The AirPods Pro 2, Apple's latest iteration of its high-performance wireless earbuds, have redefined what users can expect from portable audio devices. With powerful sound quality, exceptional noise-cancelling technology, and a range of features designed to seamlessly integrate into the Apple ecosystem, the AirPods Pro 2 provide a superior listening experience across a wide variety of use cases. In this final chapter, we will reflect on how the AirPods Pro 2 enhance daily life, providing real-world examples of their impact, and offer guidance on how to keep your AirPods in optimal condition for long-term use, ensuring that you get the most out of these premium earbuds.

How AirPods Pro 2 Enhance Your Daily Life

For many users, the AirPods Pro 2 have become an essential part of their daily routine. From making phone calls to listening to music, podcasts, and audiobooks, the versatility of these earbuds is unmatched. Their integration with Apple devices, combined with advanced features like Active Noise Cancellation (ANC), Transparency Mode, and Spatial Audio, makes them not only a luxury but also a tool that can enhance productivity, focus, and enjoyment in daily life. Below, we will examine how AirPods Pro 2 have impacted users in real-world scenarios.

Personal Testimonials or Real-World Examples of How Users Benefit from the AirPods Pro 2

Example 1: A Commuter's Best Friend
For many people who commute daily, AirPods Pro 2 are more than just a convenience – they are a lifeline. Take Sarah, for instance, a 35-year-old marketing manager who spends an hour commuting each way. She often found it difficult to enjoy her music or podcasts due to the constant noise from the crowded subway trains and bustling city streets. After switching to the AirPods Pro 2, Sarah was amazed at the difference ANC made in blocking out the noisy environment. Not only could she enjoy her music without distraction, but she also found that she could tune out the stress of her daily commute and arrive at work feeling more focused and relaxed. Additionally, the ability to switch seamlessly from her iPhone to her MacBook, thanks to automatic device switching, made her commute even more productive.

Example 2: A Fitness Enthusiast's Workout Companion

James, a 28-year-old fitness enthusiast, had always struggled to find a pair of earbuds that could stay secure during his intense workouts. He would often worry about his previous wireless earbuds falling out during high-impact activities like running or cycling. After trying the AirPods Pro 2, James was thrilled with the **customizable fit** of the silicone ear tips, which provided a secure seal and helped deliver excellent sound quality. Whether he was running on the treadmill or cycling outdoors, the AirPods Pro 2 stayed in place and provided immersive sound, especially with ANC, which allowed him to focus on his workout without distractions. Furthermore, the sweat and water resistance of the AirPods Pro 2 meant that he could work out with peace of mind, knowing his earbuds were protected from moisture.

Example 3: A Professional's Efficient Work Tool

Daniel, a 42-year-old software developer, spends most of his workday on video calls and virtual meetings. While he initially relied on traditional wired headphones, he switched to the AirPods Pro 2 after hearing about their advanced microphone technology and ANC features. He quickly noticed that the sound quality during calls was incredibly clear, thanks to the **adaptive beamforming microphones** that isolate his voice while minimizing background noise. Whether in his office or on-the-go, Daniel could rely on his AirPods to make sure his calls sounded professional and free from distractions. Additionally, the **seamless integration with his MacBook** allowed him to switch between calls, music, and podcast listening effortlessly, without missing a beat.

Example 4: A Traveler's Quiet Escape

For frequent travelers like Olivia, the AirPods Pro 2 are a game-changer. Olivia, who often travels internationally for work, needed a pair of earbuds that could block out the hum of the airplane engines and provide an immersive experience while watching movies on her iPad or listening to music. The **Active Noise Cancellation** on the AirPods Pro 2 proved invaluable, as it allowed her to escape into her content without the distraction of the airplane's noise. She also appreciated the **Transparency Mode**, which allowed her to hear important announcements from the flight crew without needing to remove her earbuds. In her downtime, Olivia used the **Spatial Audio** feature to enjoy movies with surround sound-like clarity, making her flights feel more comfortable and less isolating.

These real-world examples highlight how AirPods Pro 2 fit into various aspects of daily life, from work to fitness, travel, and leisure. The combination of sound quality, seamless connectivity, and cutting-edge features ensures that the AirPods Pro 2 can provide significant benefits across different use cases.

Reflection on the Overall Value of AirPods in Improving Audio Experiences

The AirPods Pro 2 are more than just wireless earbuds; they represent a breakthrough in personal audio technology. With each iteration of the AirPods, Apple has continually raised the bar for what users can expect from portable audio devices. Whether you're a commuter, a traveler, a fitness enthusiast, or a professional, the AirPods Pro 2 provide an exceptional experience that is hard to beat.

The **sound quality** delivered by the AirPods Pro 2 is remarkable, with deep bass, clear mids, and bright highs that make everything from music to podcasts sound vibrant and immersive. The addition of **Spatial Audio** further elevates the experience by creating a dynamic, 3D listening environment. **Active Noise Cancellation** ensures that users can enjoy their audio without interruption, whether they're in a noisy environment or simply want to block out the outside world for a few hours. Additionally, **Transparency Mode** offers the perfect balance, allowing users to stay aware of their surroundings while still enjoying their content.

The integration of these features into the **Apple ecosystem** is another significant advantage of the AirPods Pro 2. Seamless pairing with iPhones, iPads, Macs, and even the Apple Watch ensures that you never have to worry about switching devices or connectivity issues. The AirPods Pro 2 are designed to work effortlessly across all your Apple products, enhancing the overall experience and making them an indispensable part of your daily routine.

Ultimately, the value of the AirPods Pro 2 lies in how they improve users' everyday lives. Whether it's helping you stay focused during a busy workday, providing a relaxing escape during a commute, or offering the best sound quality during your workouts, the AirPods Pro 2 elevate every audio experience. With their versatility and exceptional performance, they are undoubtedly one of the best wireless earbuds available today.

Encouraging Long-Term Care and Enjoyment

While the AirPods Pro 2 are built to last and provide an exceptional experience, proper care and maintenance are key to ensuring that they continue to perform optimally over the long term. By following simple cleaning and maintenance practices, you can extend the life of your AirPods Pro 2 and keep them functioning at their best.

How to Keep Using Your AirPods for Years to Come with Proper Care and Maintenance

To ensure that your AirPods Pro 2 remain in good condition for as long as possible, follow these care guidelines:

Clean Your AirPods Regularly: Over time, earwax, dirt, and debris can accumulate on the earbuds and inside the charging case, affecting both sound quality and comfort. To clean your AirPods Pro 2, use a **soft, lint-free cloth** to wipe down the exterior and a **dry cotton swab** to clean the charging contacts. Avoid using any harsh chemicals or abrasive materials, as these can damage the surface or internal components.

Store Your AirPods Properly: When not in use, always store your AirPods Pro 2 in the **charging case**. This helps protect them from damage and ensures they stay clean. If you're storing them in a bag or pocket, consider using a **protective case** for added protection against scratches and drops. Additionally, avoid leaving your AirPods exposed to extreme temperatures, as this can affect the battery and performance.

Maintain Battery Health: The battery life of your AirPods Pro 2 is designed to last for hundreds of charge cycles, but it's important to maintain good charging habits to preserve battery health. Avoid letting your AirPods or the charging case completely drain to 0% on a regular basis. Instead, try to charge them when they reach around 20-30% for optimal battery health. Also, enable **Optimized Battery Charging** in the **Settings** to prevent the battery from charging past 80% during prolonged periods of being plugged in.

Check for Software Updates: Regularly updating the firmware of your AirPods Pro 2 ensures that you get the latest performance improvements and bug fixes. To check for updates, simply keep your AirPods connected to your iPhone, and the updates will automatically be installed when available. You can also check the firmware version in the **Settings > Bluetooth** menu, where you can view the firmware details of your AirPods.

Monitor Your Audio Exposure: As part of Apple's commitment to hearing health, AirPods Pro 2 provide tools for tracking your audio exposure over time. Use the **Apple Health app** to monitor how much time you spend listening to audio at high volumes and make adjustments to reduce the risk of hearing damage. By following the **80/80 rule** (listening at 80% volume for no more than 80 minutes per day), you can protect your hearing while still enjoying your audio content.

Final Encouragement to Take Full Advantage of the AirPods Pro 2 Features

The AirPods Pro 2 offer an exceptional array of features that can elevate your daily life, from noise cancellation and spatial audio to seamless integration with your Apple devices. To get the most out of your AirPods, take the time to explore all the features they offer, from custom sound profiles to advanced connectivity options across devices. Don't hesitate to dive into the settings, personalize your listening experience, and experiment with different features to find what works best for you.

By caring for your AirPods Pro 2 and maintaining them properly, you can ensure that they remain a reliable and valuable part of your audio setup for years to come. The AirPods Pro 2 aren't just a product; they are an investment in your daily audio enjoyment, productivity, and overall well-being. So, take full advantage of their features, care for them with attention, and enjoy the rich sound experience they offer!

Made in the USA
Columbia, SC
19 June 2025

59630627R00065